PIANO / VOCAL / GUITAR

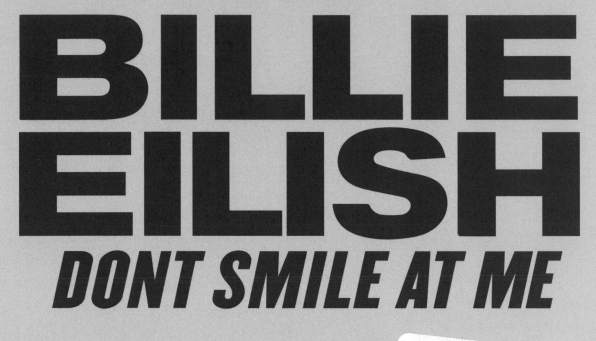

BILLIE EILISH
DONT SMILE AT ME

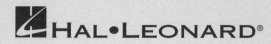

ISBN 978-1-5400-4965-0

HAL•LEONARD®

Visit Hal Leonard Online at
www.halleonard.com

Contact us:
Hal Leonard
7777 West Bluemound Road
Milwaukee, WI 53213
Email: info@halleonard.com

In Europe, contact:
Hal Leonard Europe Limited
42 Wigmore Street
Marylebone, London, W1U 2RN
Email: info@halleonardeurope.com

In Australia, contact:
Hal Leonard Australia Pty. Ltd.
4 Lentara Court
Cheltenham, Victoria, 3192 Australia
Email: info@halleonard.com.au

COPYCAT

Words and Music by BILLIE EILISH
and FINNEAS O'CONNELL

5

Per - fect mur - der, take your aim. I don't be - long to an - y - one but ev -'ry - bod - y knows my __ name.

By the way, you've been un - in - vit - ed 'cause all you say

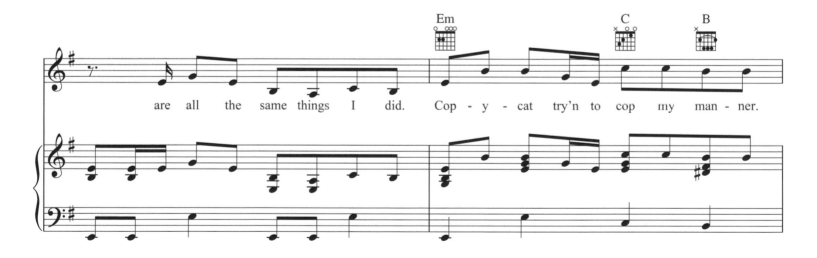

are all the same things I did. Cop - y - cat try'n to cop my man - ner.

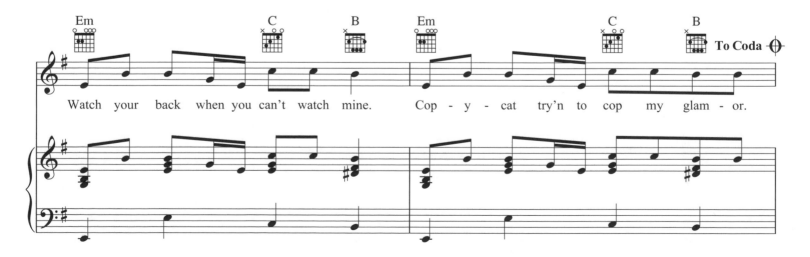

Watch your back when you can't watch mine. Cop - y - cat try'n to cop my glam - or.

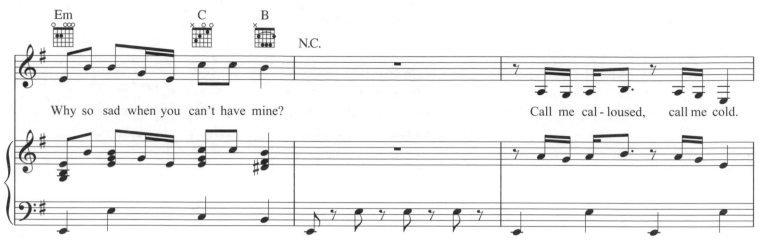

Why so sad when you can't have mine? Call me cal-loused, call me cold.

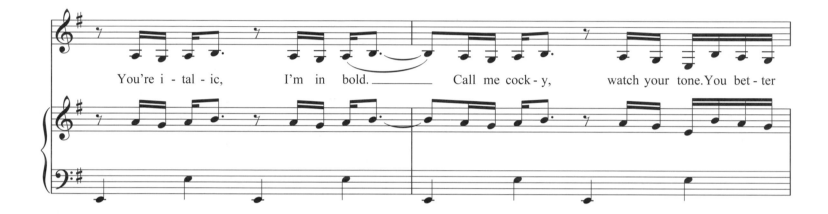

You're i - tal - ic, I'm in bold. _____ Call me cock - y, watch your tone. You bet - ter

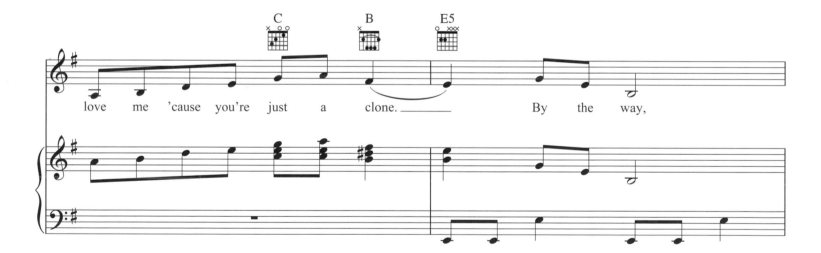

love me 'cause you're just a clone. _____ By the way,

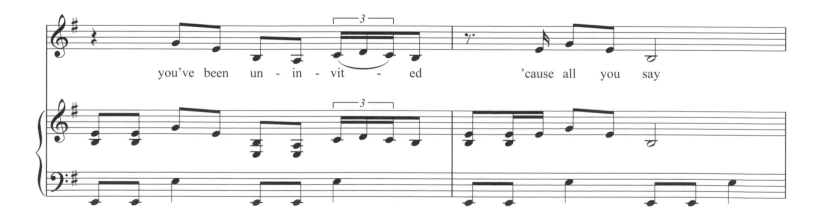

you've been un - in - vit - ed 'cause all you say

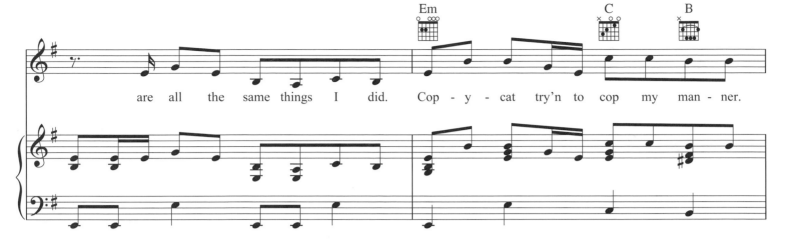

are all the same things I did. Cop - y - cat try'n to cop my man - ner.

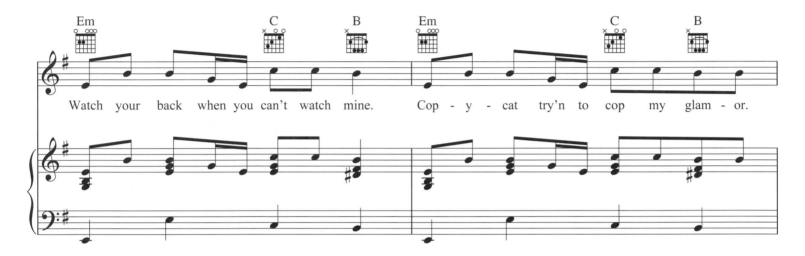

Watch your back when you can't watch mine. Cop - y - cat try'n to cop my glam - or.

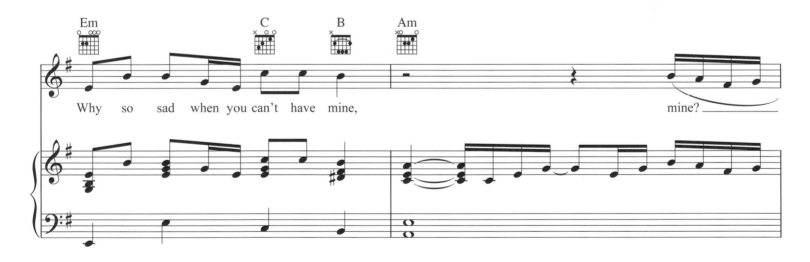

Why so sad when you can't have mine, mine? _____

_____ I would hate to see you go. _____ Hate to be the

8

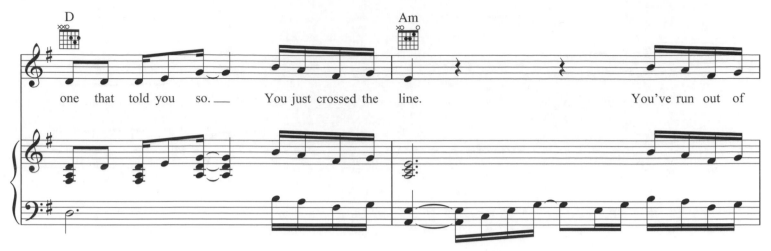

one that told you so. __ You just crossed the line. You've run out of

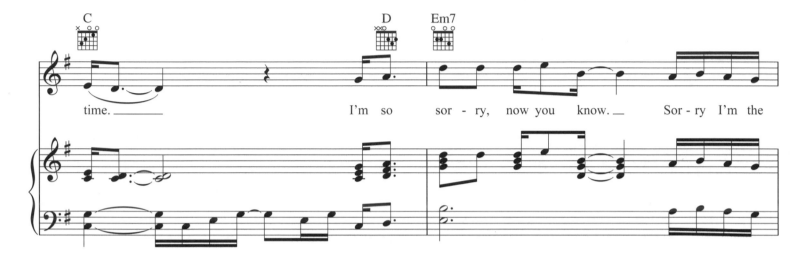

time. _____ I'm so sor - ry, now you know. __ Sor - ry I'm the

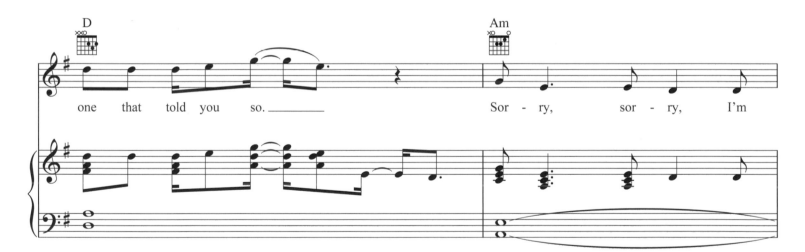

one that told you so. _____ Sor - ry, sor - ry, I'm

D.S. al Coda

sor - ry, sor - ry, psych.

CODA

Why so sad when you can't have mine?

idontwannabeyouanymore

Words and Music by BILLIE EILISH
and FINNEAS O'CONNELL

Slowly, in 2

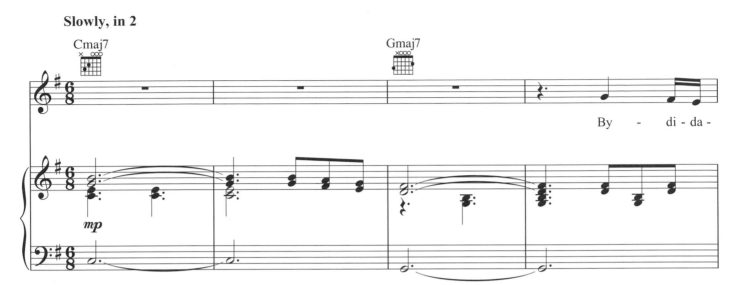

By - di - da -

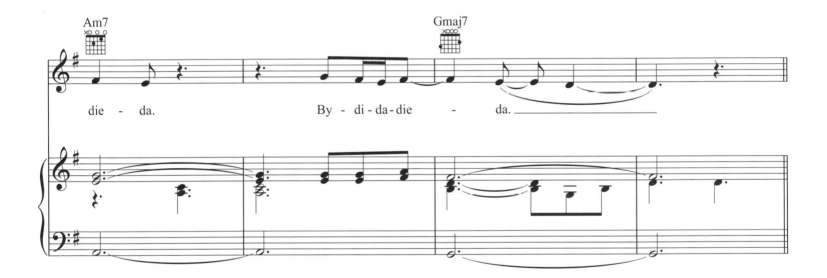

die - da.   By - di - da - die - da.

Don't   be that way,   fall a - part _____ twice a day.   I just

wish you could feel what you say.

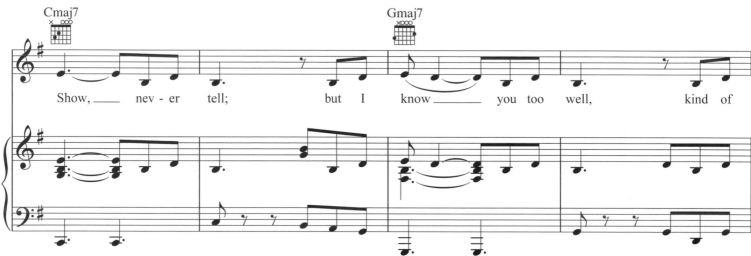

Show, _____ nev - er tell; but I know _____ you too well, kind of

mood _____ that you wish you could _____ sell. _ If

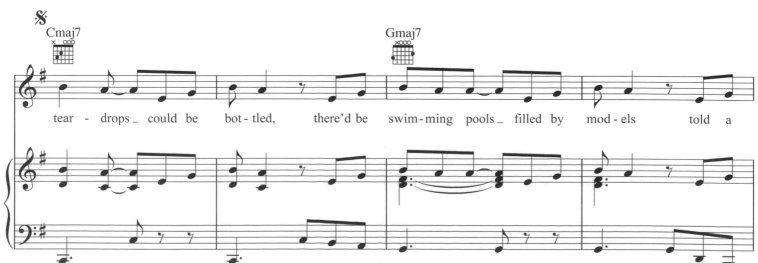

tear - drops _ could be bot - tled, there'd be swim - ming pools _ filled by mod - els told a

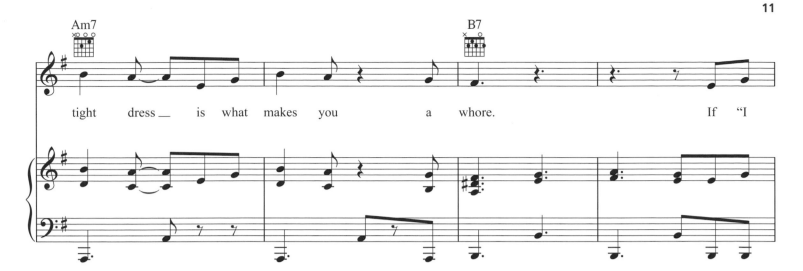

tight dress __ is what makes you a whore. If "I

love you" was a prom- ise, would you break it ___ if you're hon- est, tell the

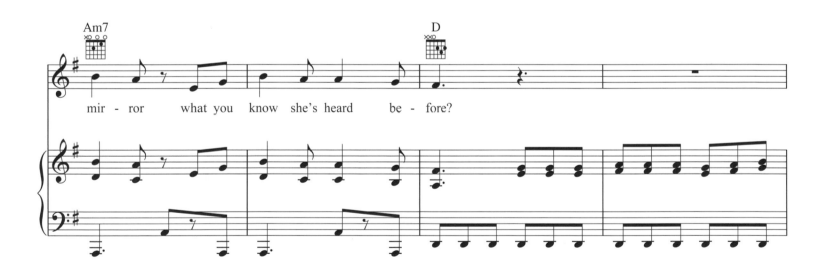

mir - ror what you know she's heard be - fore?

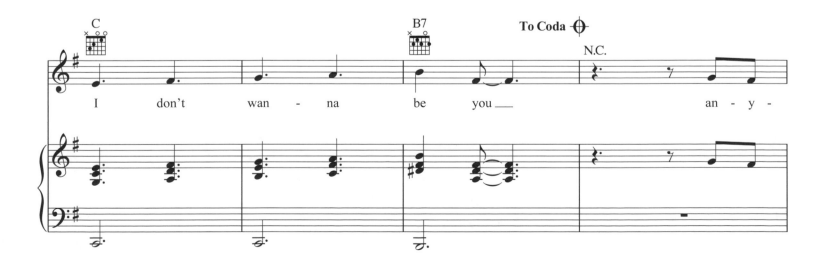

I don't wan - na be you ___ an - y-

more. _____

Hands _____ get-ting cold, los - ing feel - ing is get-ting old. _ Was I

made _____ from a bro - ken _____ mold? _____

Hurt I can't shake, we've made ev - 'ry mis - take. On - ly

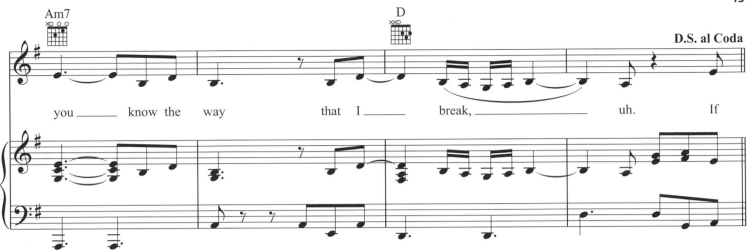

D.S. al Coda

you ____ know the way   that I ____ break, _____ uh.   If

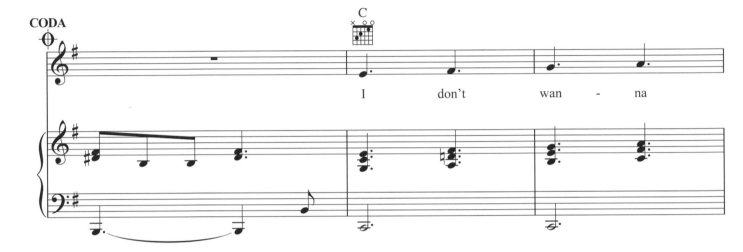

CODA

I   don't   wan -   na

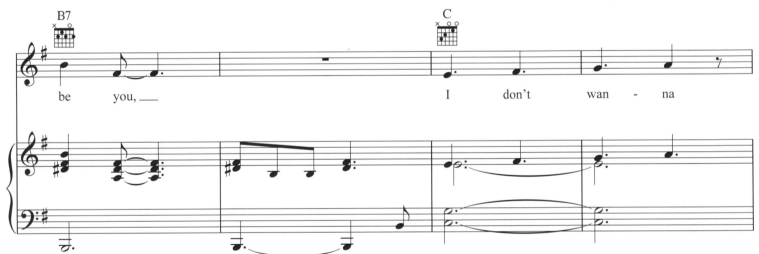

be   you, ___   I   don't   wan -   na

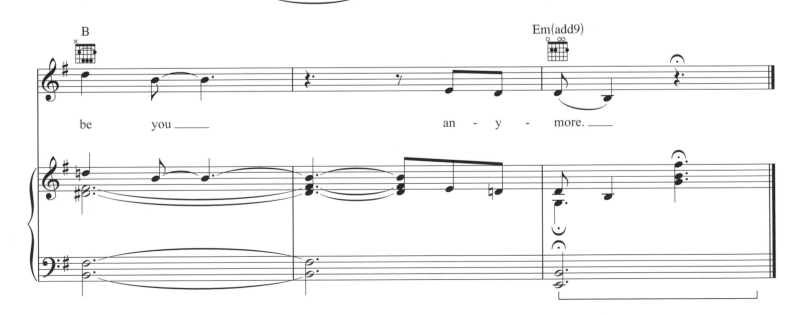

be   you ____   an - y - more. ____

MY BOY

Words and Music by BILLIE EILISH
and FINNEAS O'CONNELL

Moderately slow

Bah, boo dah. _____ Ba, boo, dah, boo, dah, _____

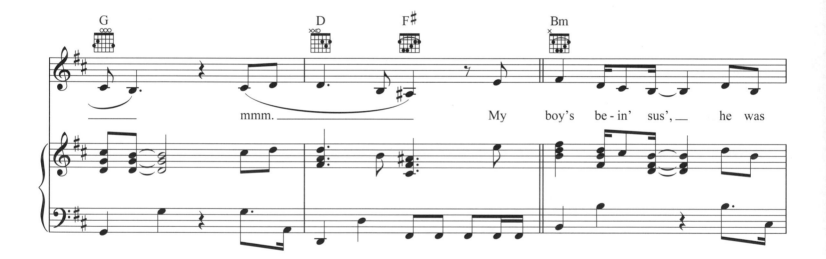

mmm. _____ My boy's be-in' sus', _____ he was

sha-dy e-nough but now he's just a sha - dow. My

boy loves his friends_ like I ___ love my split ends and by that I mean ___ he cuts them off.

Faster groove

What? My boy, my boy, my boy ___ don't

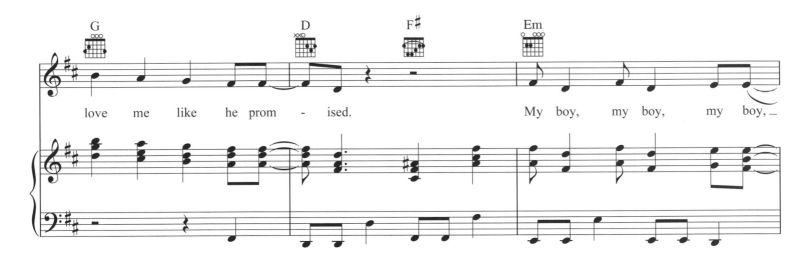

love me like he prom - ised. My boy, my boy, my boy, _

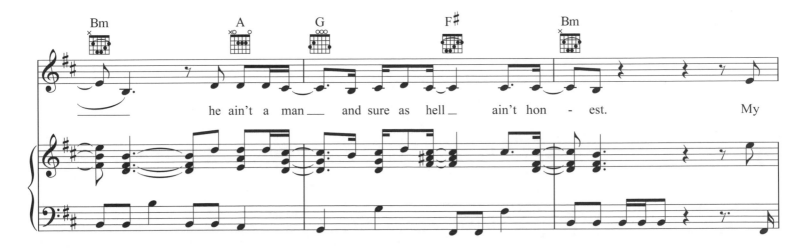

___ he ain't a man ___ and sure as hell _ ain't hon - est. My

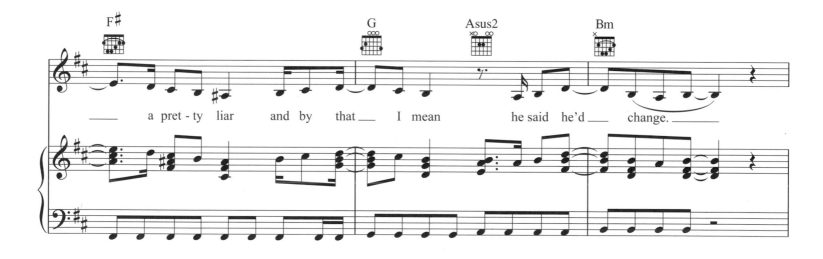

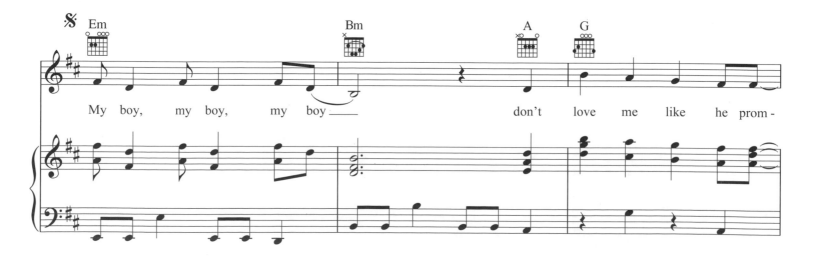

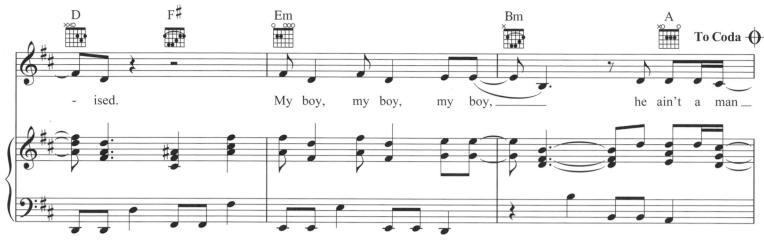

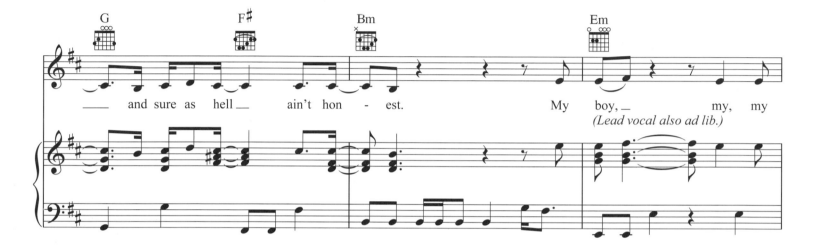

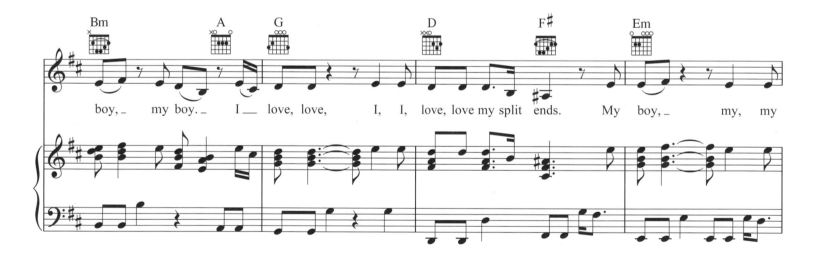

CODA

_____ and sure as hell _____ ain't hon - est. You

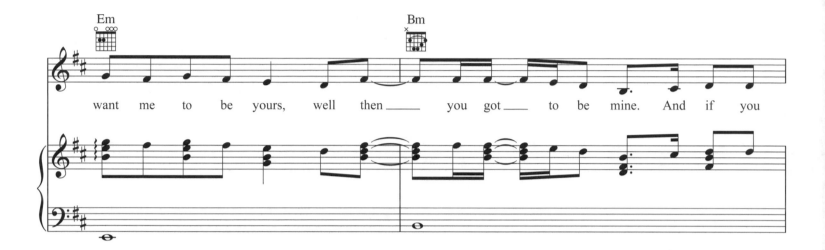

want me to be yours, well then _____ you got _____ to be mine. And if you

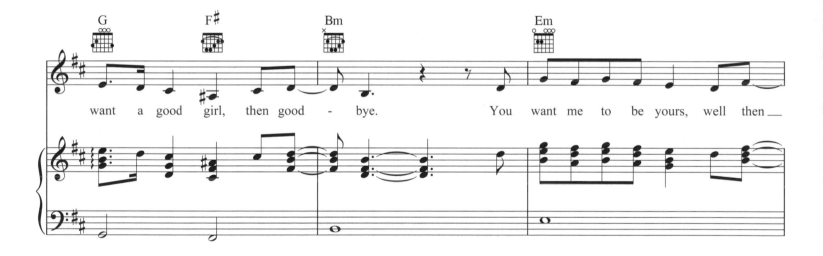

want a good girl, then good - bye. You want me to be yours, well then _____

_____ you've got - ta be mine. And if you want a good girl, then good - bye.

WATCH

Words and Music by
FINNEAS O'CONNELL

Moderate Pop groove

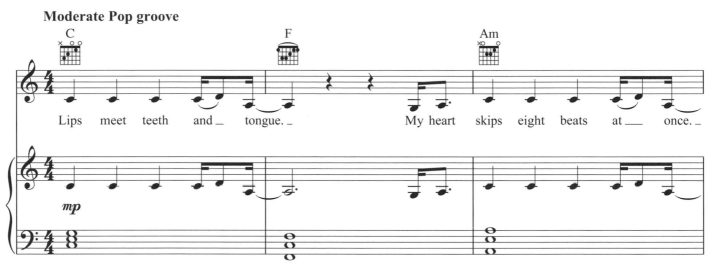

Lips meet teeth and ___ tongue. ___ My heart skips eight beats at ___ once. ___

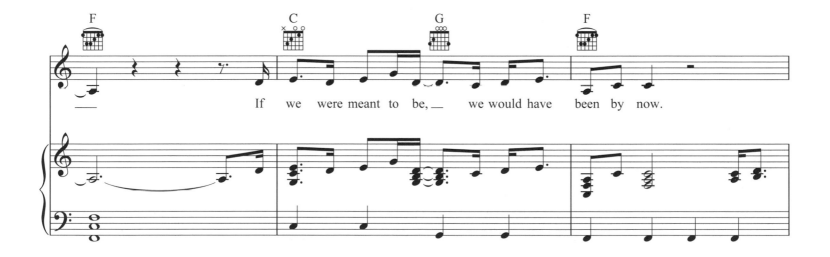

If we were meant to be, ___ we would have been by now.

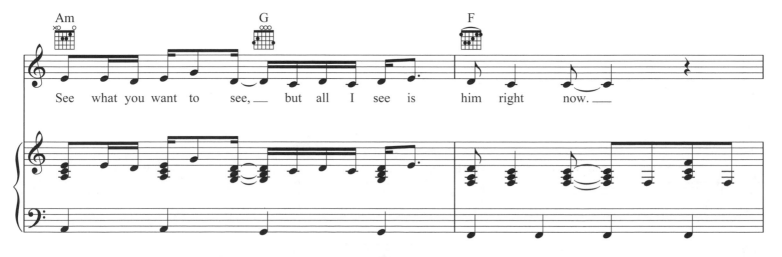

See what you want to see, ___ but all I see is him right now. ___

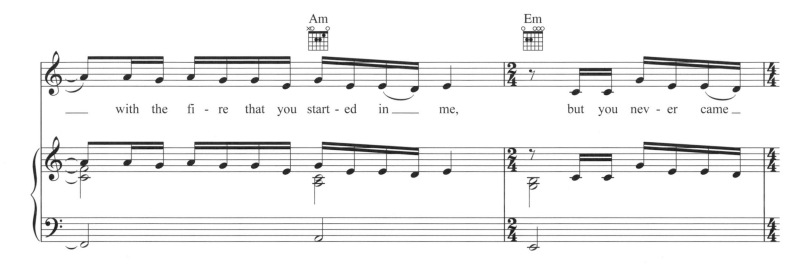

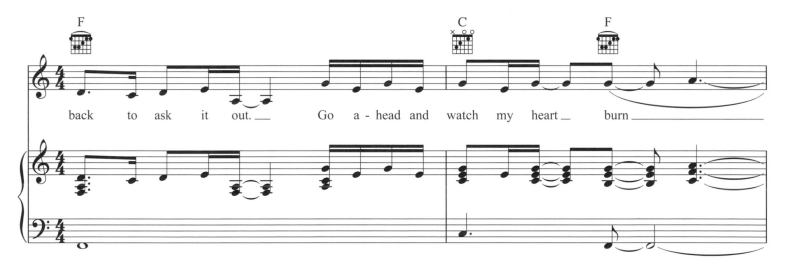

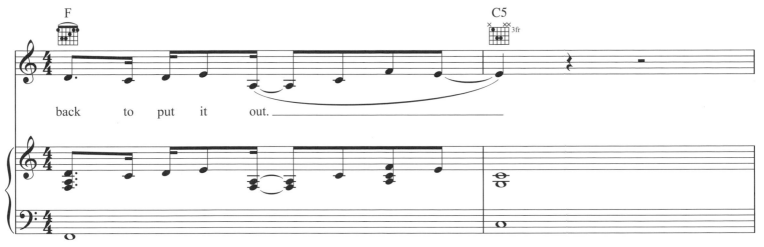

back to put it out. _____

Your love _ feels so fake _____ and my de - mands _

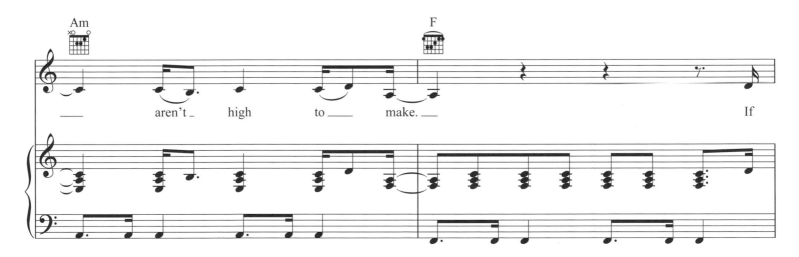

___ aren't _ high to ___ make. ___ If

I could get to sleep, _ I would have slept by now. Your

lies will nev-er keep, ___ I think you need to blow them ___ out. ___

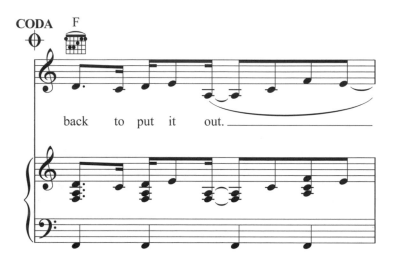

I'll sit and

back to put it out. ___

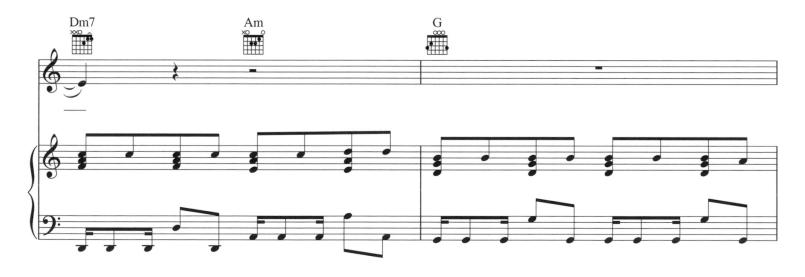

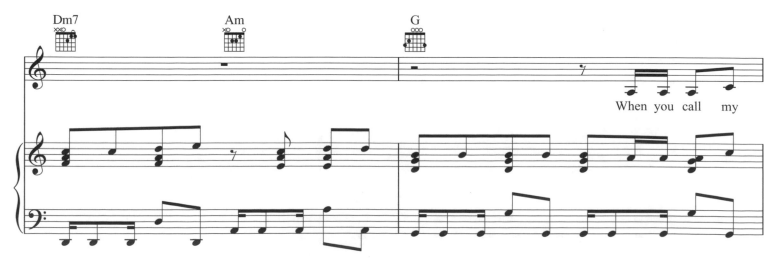

When you call my

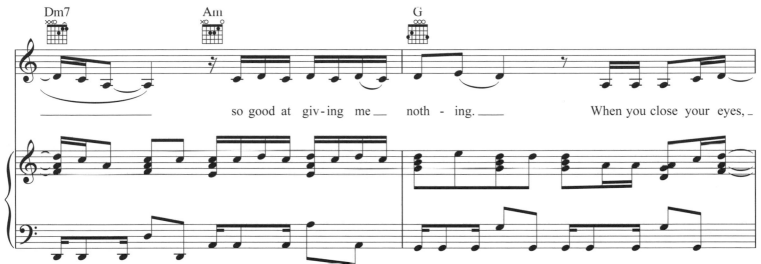

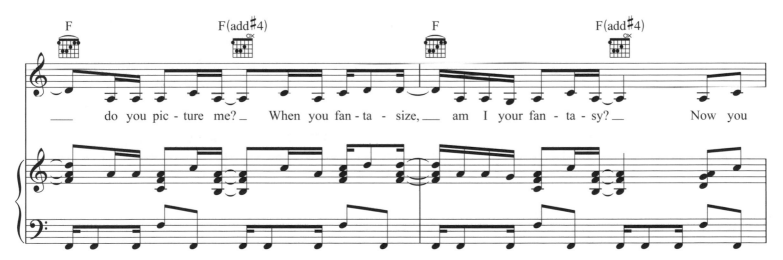

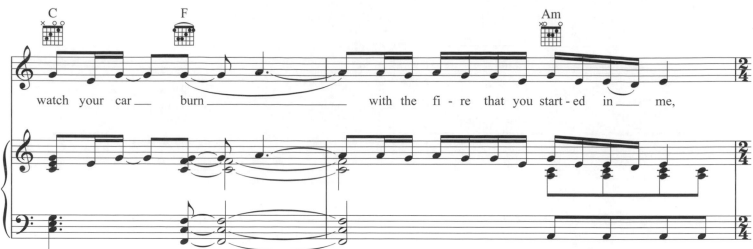

watch your car __ burn _____ with the fi - re that you start-ed in __ me,

but you nev-er came __ back to ask it out. __

Watch my heart __ burn _____ with the fi - re that you start-ed in __ me,

but I'll nev-er let you back to put it out. _____

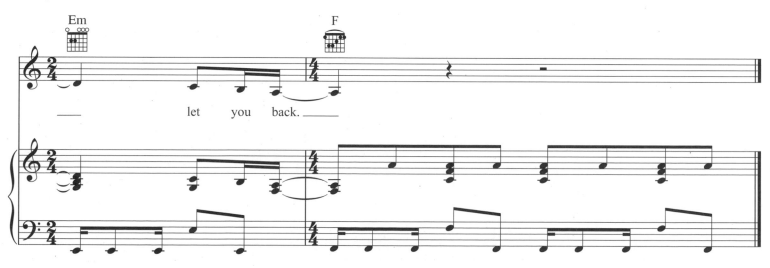

PARTY FAVOR

Words and Music by BILLIE EILISH
and FINNEAS O'CONNELL

Folky Swing

Hey,   call me back   when you get
Look,   now I know   we could have done it

_____ this   or when you've got a
bet - ter   but we can't change the

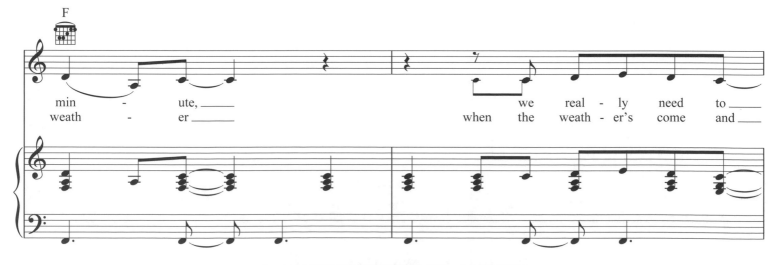

min - ute, _____   we real - ly need to _____
weath - er _____   when the weath - er's come and _____

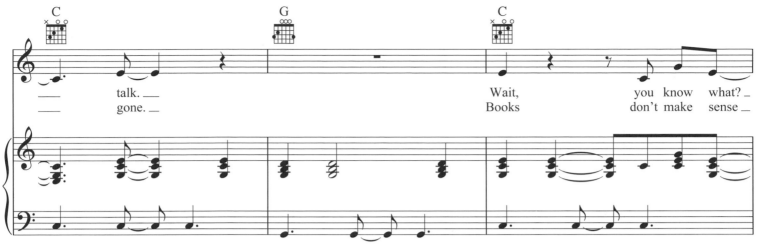

talk.
gone.

Wait,   you know what? __
Books   don't make sense __

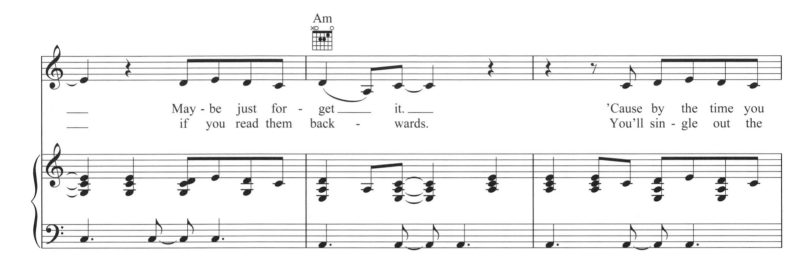

May - be just for - get __ it. __
if you read them back - wards.

'Cause by the time you
You'll sin - gle out the

get __ this, __
wrong __ words __

your num - ber might be __
like you mis - hear all my __

blocked. __
songs. __

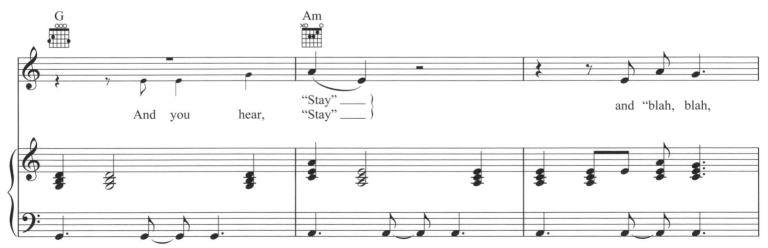

And you hear,   "Stay" __
           "Stay" __

and "blah, blah,

blah." You just want what _

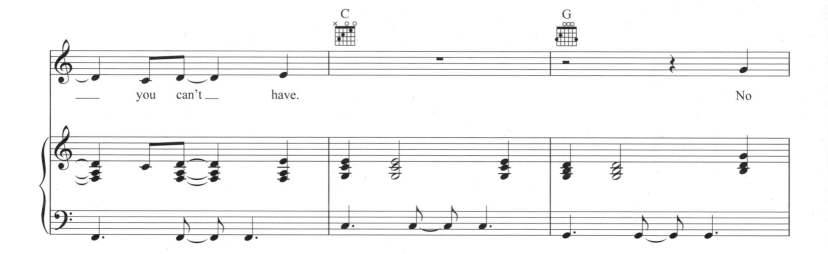

_ you can't _ have. No

way, _ I'll call the _ cops.

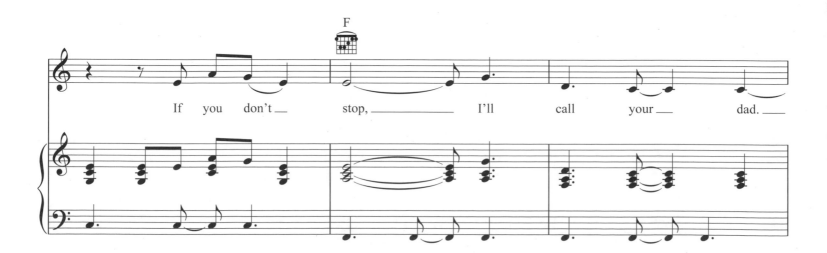

If you don't _ stop, _ I'll call your _ dad. _

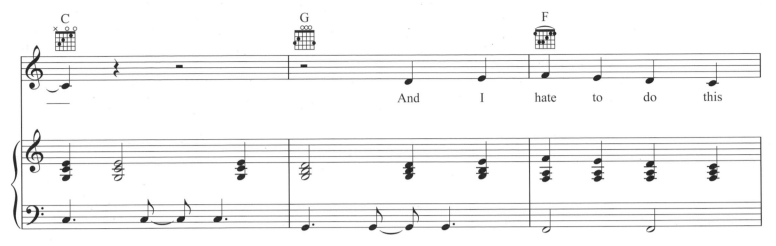

And I hate to do this

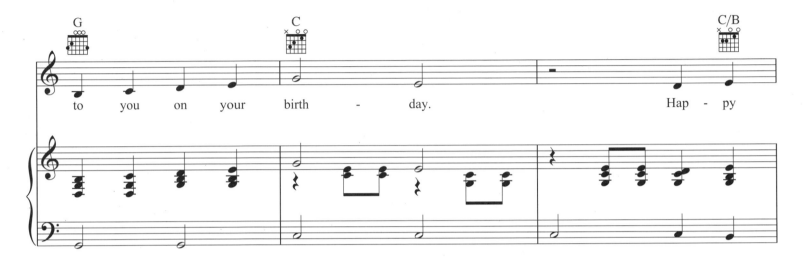

to you on your birth - day. Hap - py

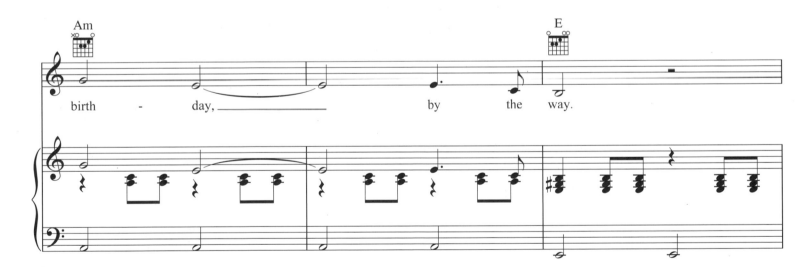

birth - day, _____ by the way.

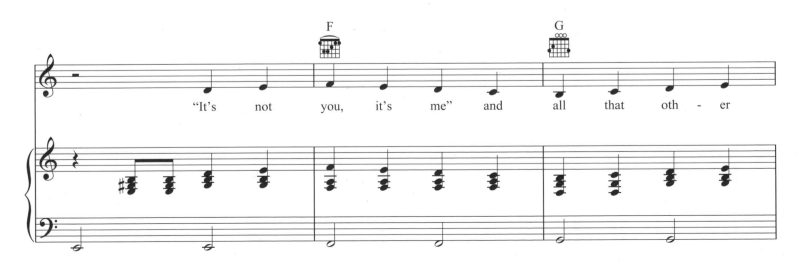

"It's not you, it's me" and all that oth - er

bull - shit. You know that's bull - shit

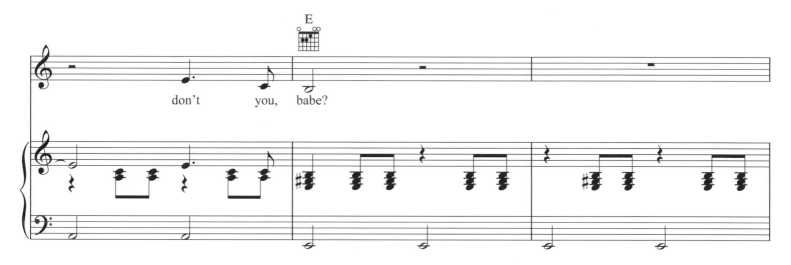

don't you, babe?

I'm not your par - ty fa - vor.

I'm not your par - ty fa - vor.

BELLYACHE

Words and Music by BILLIE EILISH
and FINNEAS O'CONNELL

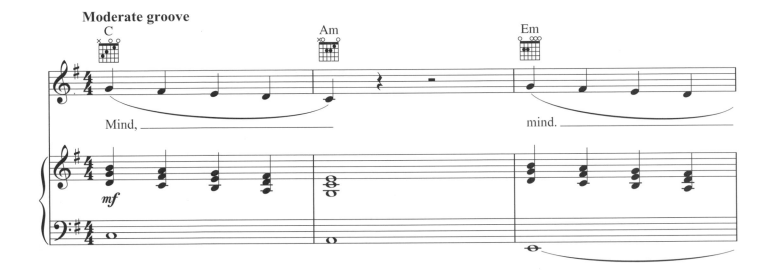

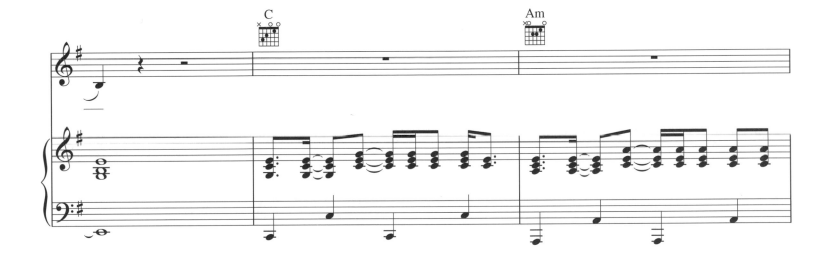

mouth full of gum _____ in the drive - way. My

friends are - n't _____ far, _____ in the back of my car _____ lay their

bod - ies. Where's my mind? _____

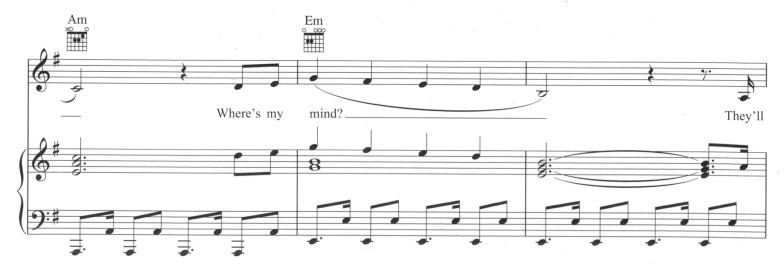

_____ Where's my mind? _____ They'll

mind? / mind. _____ Where's my mind? _____

Where's __ my mind? _____ May-be it's in the

gut-ter _____ where I __ left my lov-er. _____ What an ex-pen-sive ___ fate.

My V is for Ven-det-ta. _____ Thought that I'd __ feel bet-ter _____ and now I've got a bel-ly-ache.

To Coda ⊕

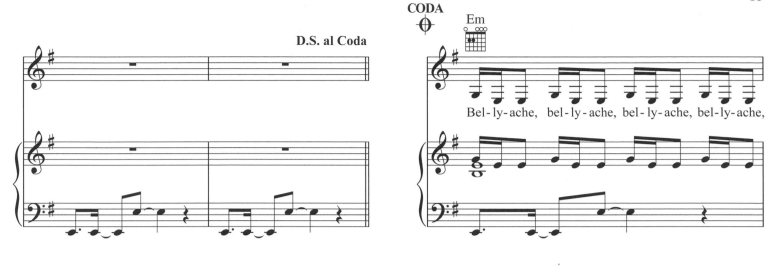

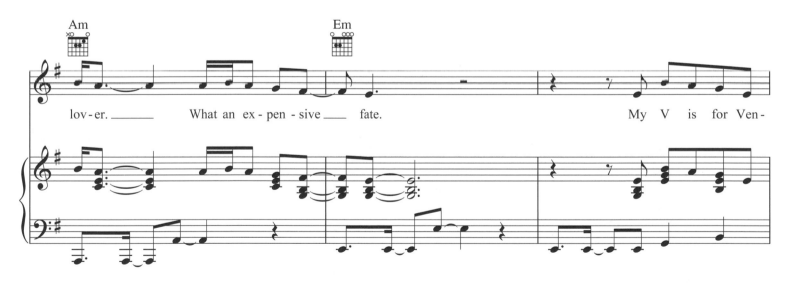

OCEAN EYES

Words and Music by
FINNEAS O'CONNELL

Ahh, _____ ahh, _____ ahh, _____

ahh. _____ I've been_ watch - ing you for some_ time. _

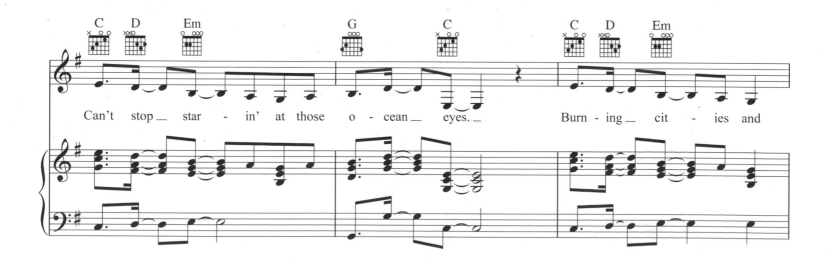

Can't stop_ star - in' at those o - cean_ eyes. _ Burn - ing_ cit - ies and

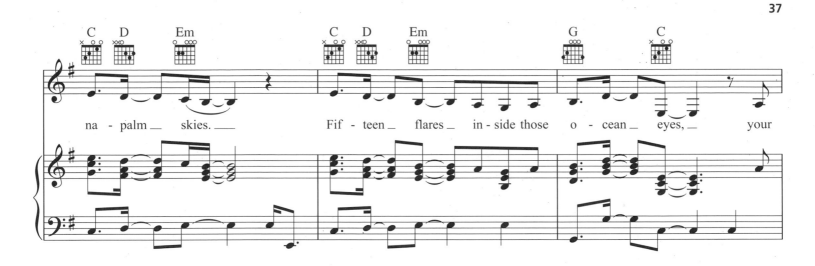

na-palm skies. Fif-teen flares in-side those o-cean eyes, your

o-cean eyes. No fair.

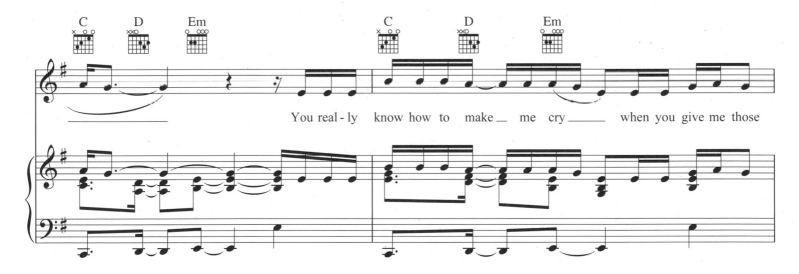

You real-ly know how to make me cry when you give me those

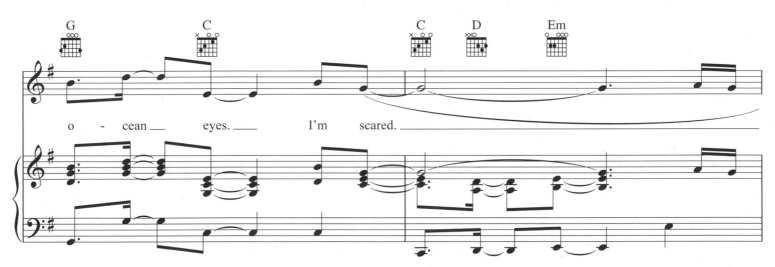

o-cean eyes. I'm scared.

I've nev-er fall-en from quite_ this high.____ Fall-ing in-to your

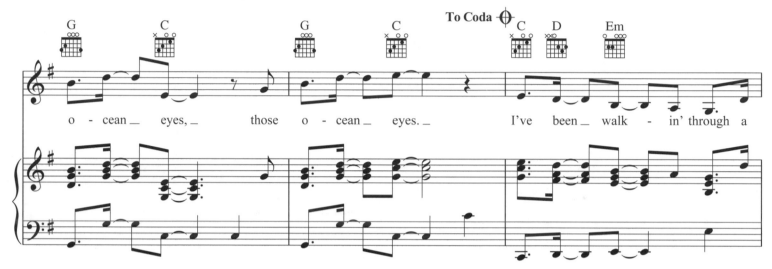

o - cean_ eyes,_ those o - cean_ eyes._ I've been_ walk - in' through a

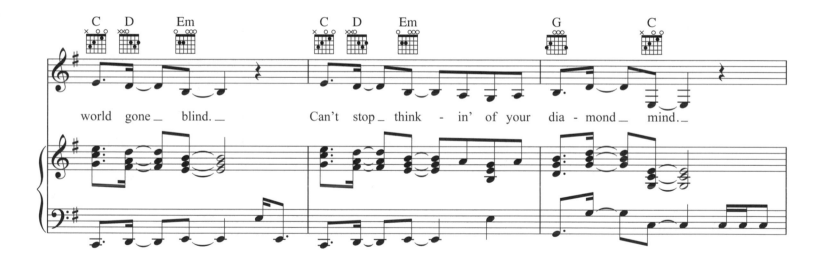

world gone_ blind._ Can't stop_ think - in' of your dia - mond_ mind._

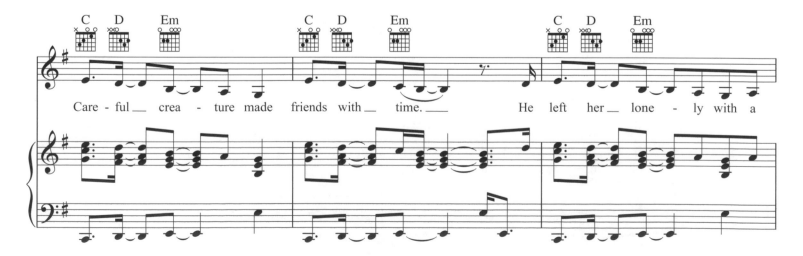

Care - ful_ crea - ture made friends with_ time.___ He left her_ lone - ly with a

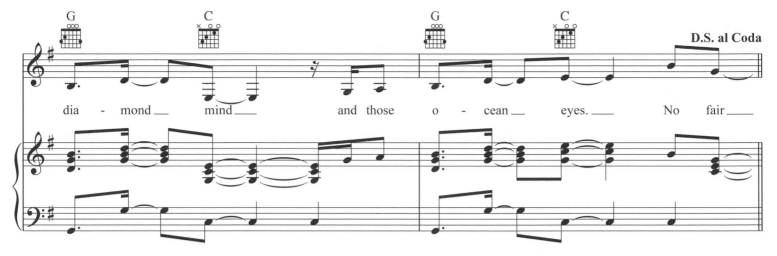

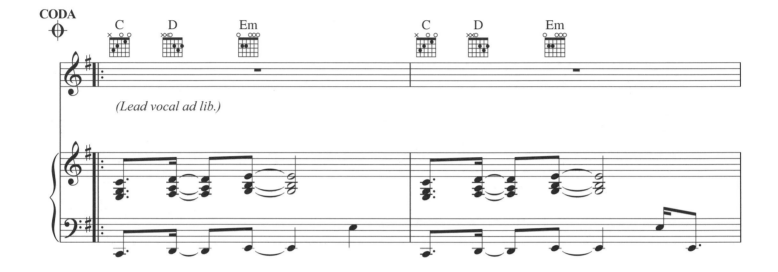

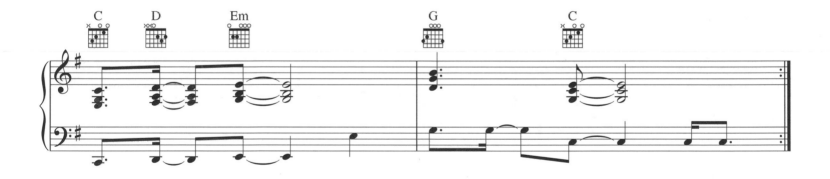

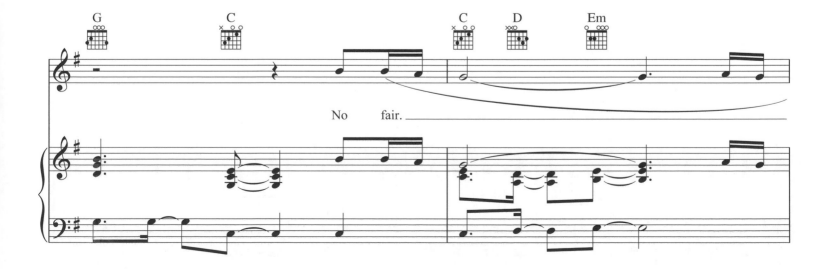

You real-ly know how to make me cry when you give me those

o - cean eyes. I'm scared.

I've nev-er fall-en quite this high. Fall-in' in-to your

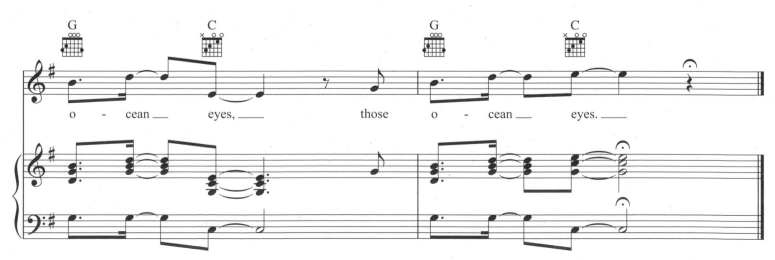

o - cean eyes, those o - cean eyes.

&BURN

Words and Music by FINNEAS O'CONNELL
and VINCE STAPLES

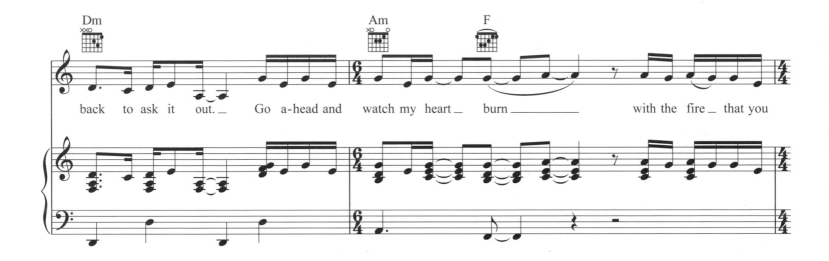

If I could get to sleep, I would have slept by now. Ahh,__ your

D.S. al Coda

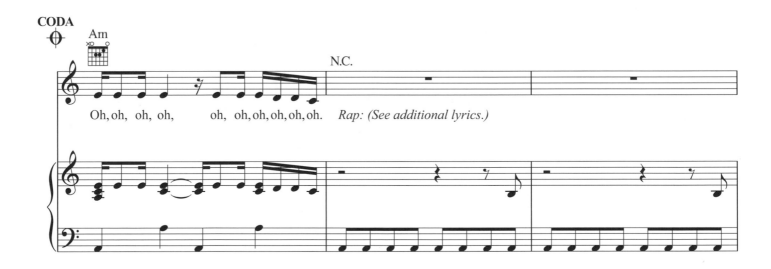

lies will nev - er keep. I think you need to blow them __ out, __ b - b - blow them __ out. __ I'll sit and

CODA

Am

N.C.

Oh, oh, oh, oh, oh, oh, oh, oh, oh, oh. *Rap: (See additional lyrics.)*

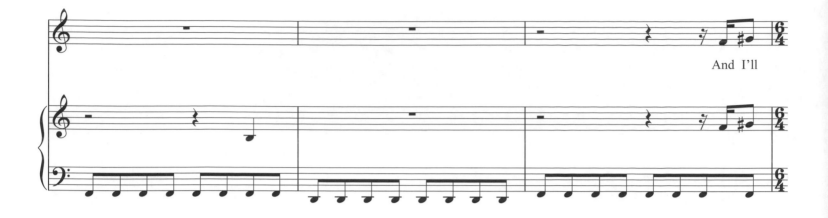

And I'll

watch your car __ burn __ with the fire __ that you start-ed in me. But you nev-er came

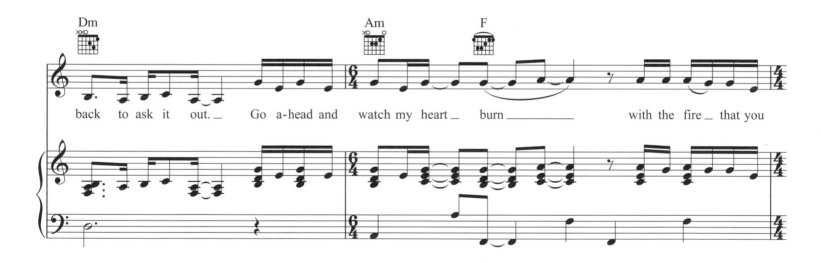

back to ask it out. __ Go a-head and watch my heart __ burn _____ with the fire __ that you

start-ed in me. _____ But I'll nev-er let you back to put it out. _____

Additional Lyrics

Rap: 7-4-2008, I still remember that. Heaven sent a present my way.
I won't forget your laugh. Packin' everything when you leave.
You know you comin' back. Wanna see me down on my knees but that
was made for a ring. I try to wait for the storm to calm down but that's stubborn, baby.
Leadin' the war, we drawn down on each other. Try'n to even the score.
We all been found guilty in the court of aorta.

HOSTAGE

Words and Music by BILLIE EILISH
and FINNEAS O'CONNELL

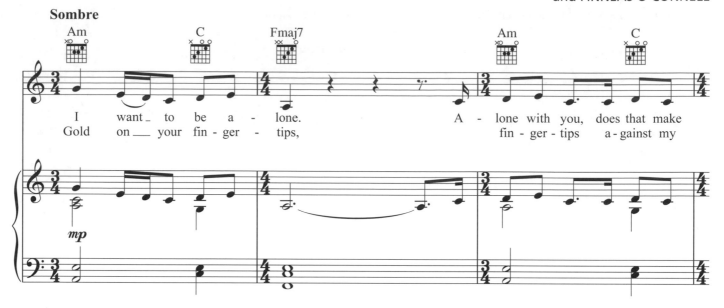

I want to be a - lone.
Gold on your fin-ger-tips,

A - lone with you, does that make
fin-ger-tips a-gainst my

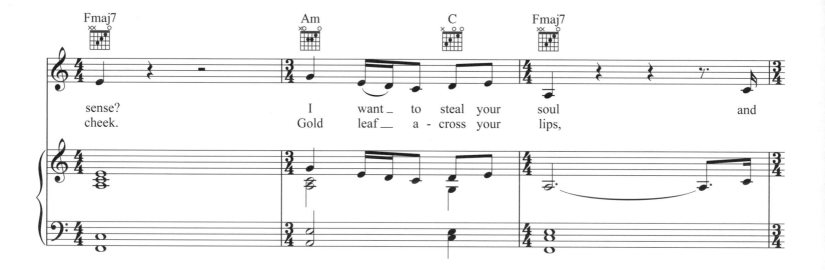

sense?
cheek.

I want to steal your soul
Gold leaf a-cross your lips,

and

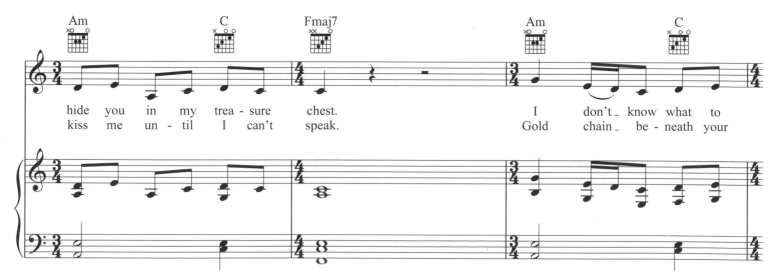

hide you in my trea-sure chest.
kiss me un-til I can't speak.

I don't know what to
Gold chain be-neath your

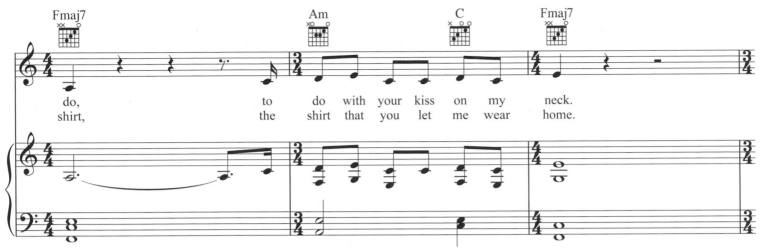

do,
shirt,
to do with your kiss on my neck.
the shirt that you let me wear home.

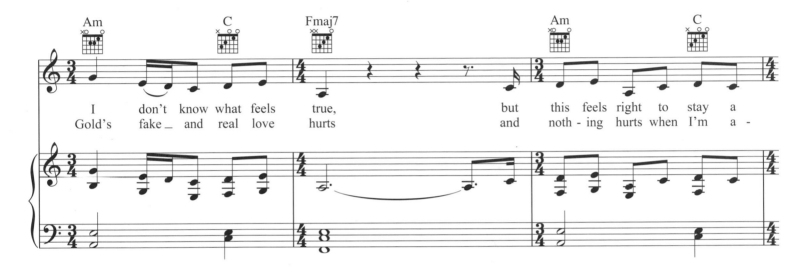

I don't know what feels true,
Gold's fake _ and real love hurts
but this feels right to stay a
and noth-ing hurts when I'm a-

sec.
lone.
Yeah, you feel right, so stay a sec.
When you're with me and we're a - lone.
And let me

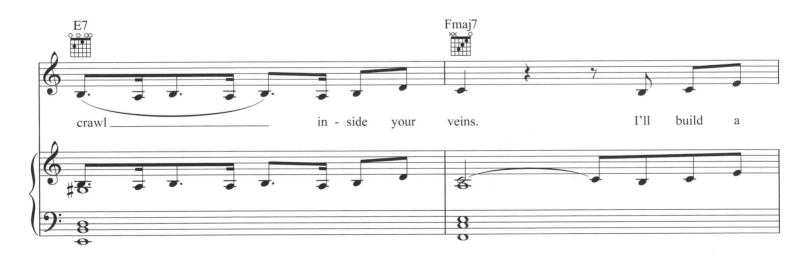

crawl _____ in - side your veins.
I'll build a

wall, _____ give you a ball and chain. It's not like

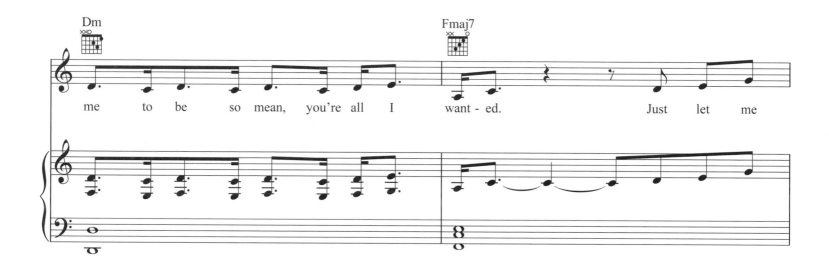

me to be so mean, you're all I want-ed. Just let me

hold _____ you like a hos - tage. _

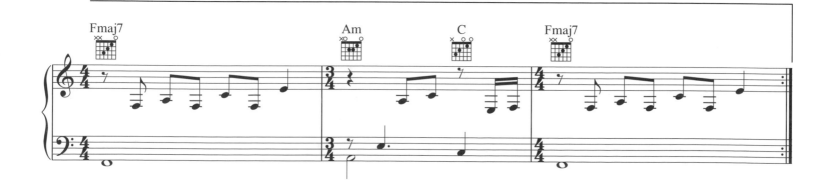

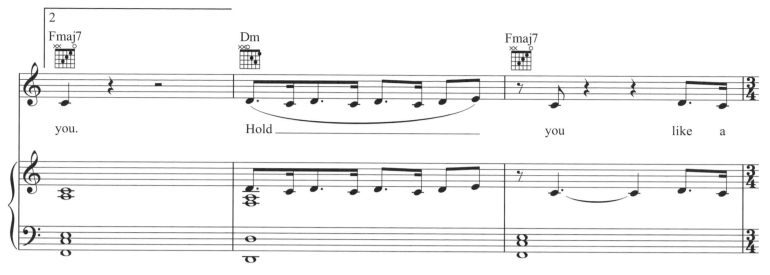

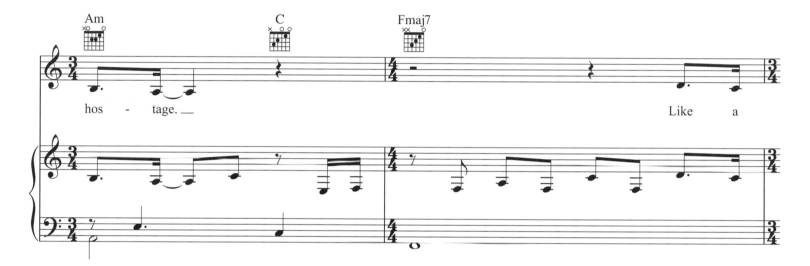

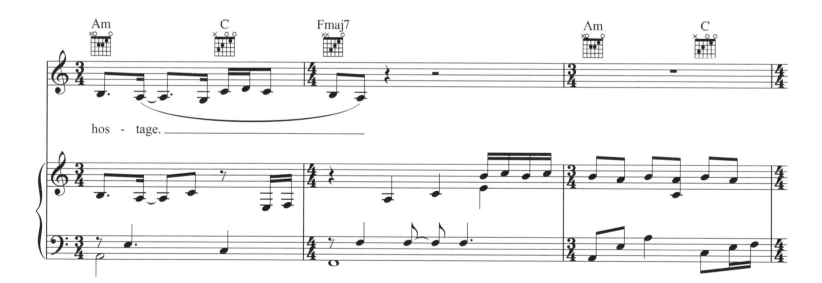

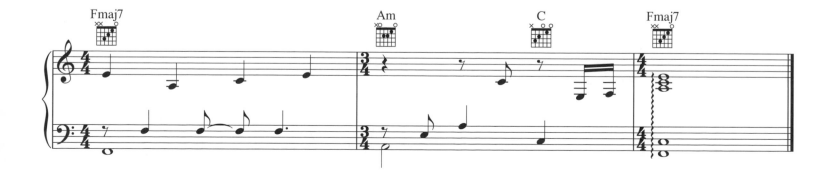

LOVELY

Words and Music by BILLIE EILISH,
FINNEAS O'CONNELL and KHALID ROBINSON

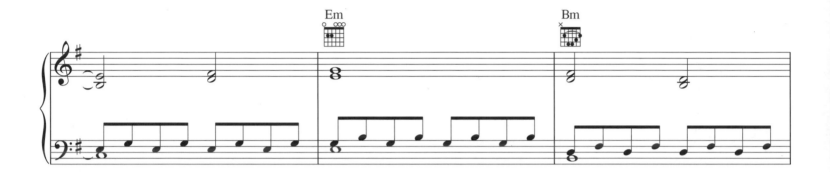

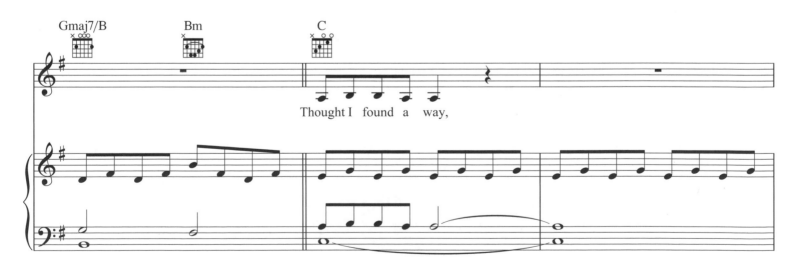

Thought I found a way,

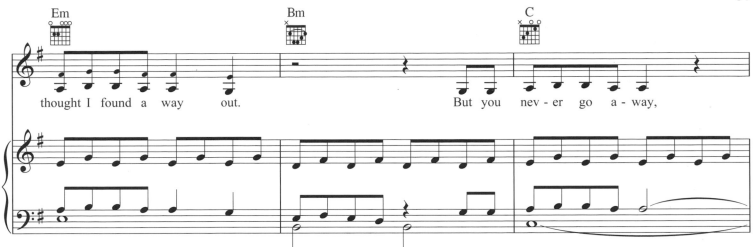

thought I found a way out. But you nev - er go a - way,

so I guess I got - ta stay now. Oh, I hope __ some -

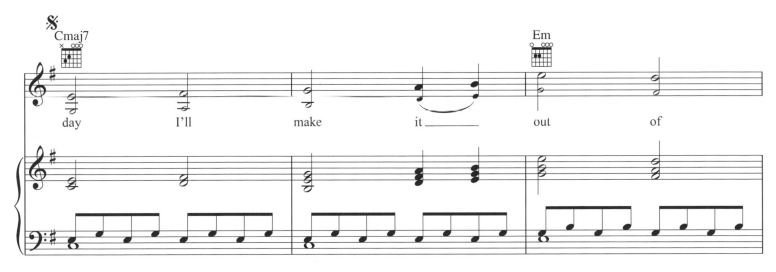

day I'll make it _____ out of

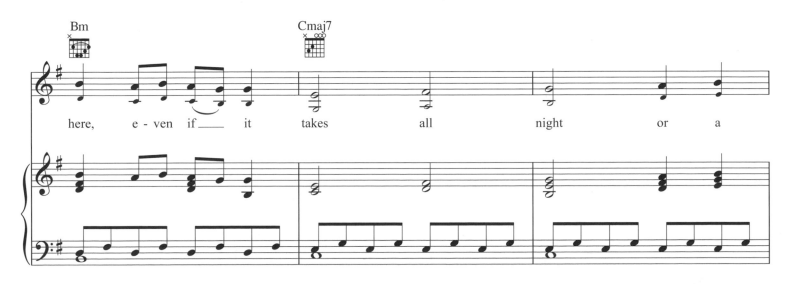

here, e - ven if ___ it takes all night or a

hun - dred years. Need a place _ to hide, but

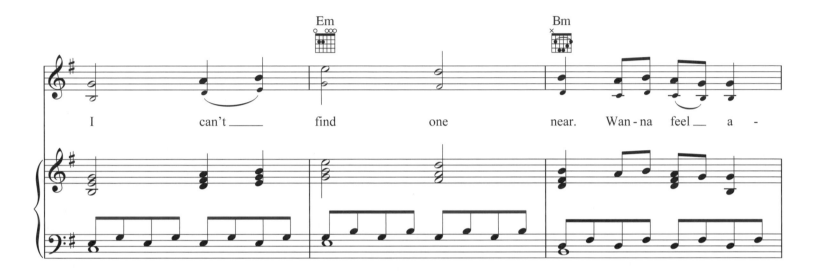

I can't _____ find one near. Wan - na feel _ a -

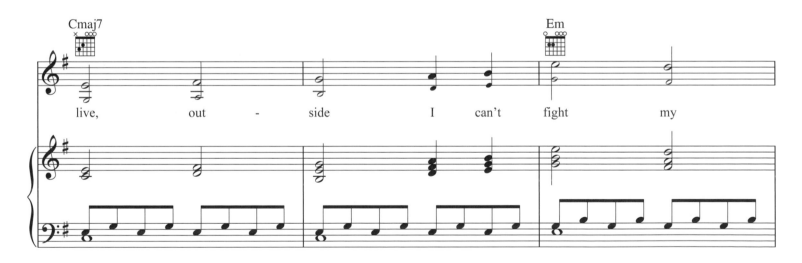

live, out - side I can't fight my

fear. Is - n't it love - ly, all a - lone?

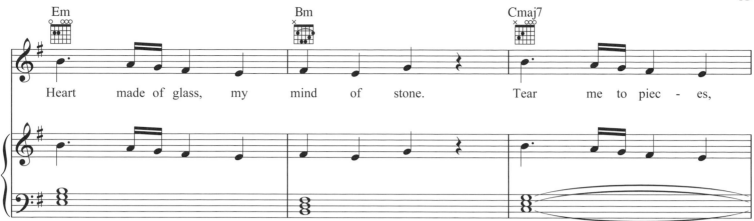

Heart made of glass, my mind of stone. Tear me to piec - es,

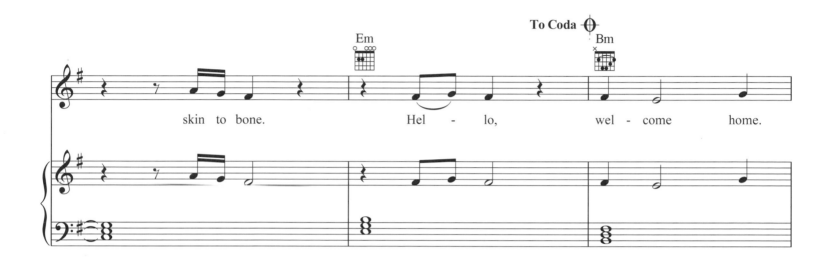

skin to bone. Hel - lo, wel - come home.

Walk-ing out of time,____

look-ing for a bet - ter place.

Some-thing's on my mind,

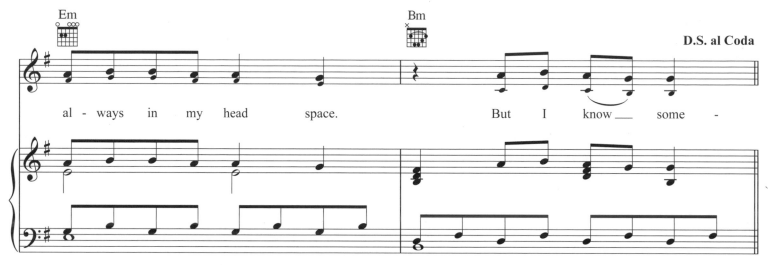

D.S. al Coda

al - ways in my head space. But I know ___ some -

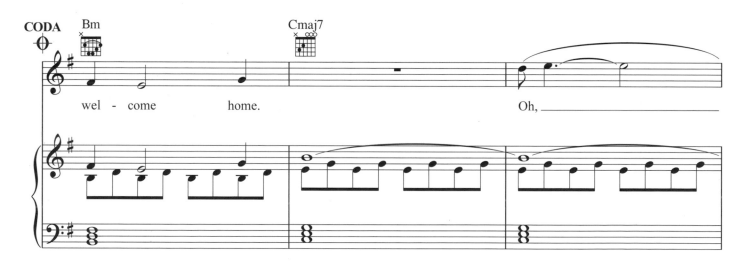

CODA

wel - come home. Oh, ___

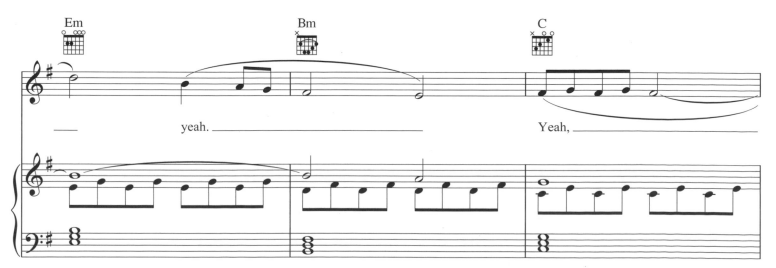

___ yeah. ___ Yeah, ___

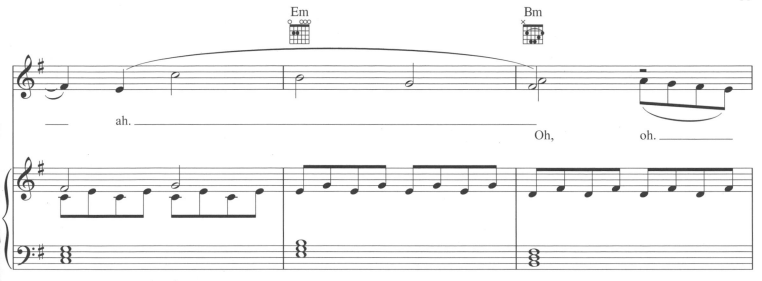

ah. Oh, oh.

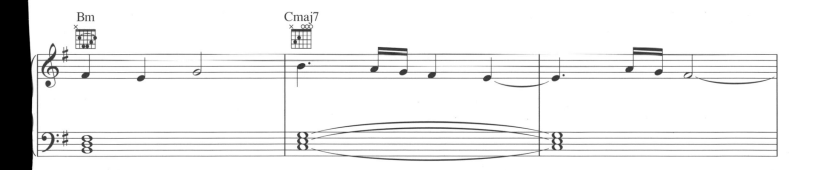

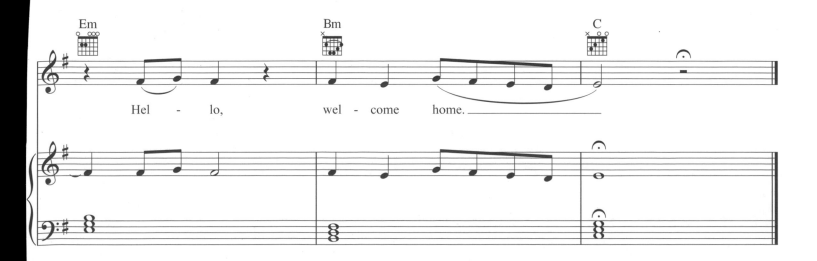

Hel - lo, wel - come home.

MORE FROM YOUR FAVORITE ARTISTS

CAMILA CABELLO – CAMILA

All ten tracks from the 2018 debut album by this Fifth Harmony alum which debuted at the top of the Billboard® 200 album charts. Our folio includes piano/vocal/guitar arrangements for the hit single "Havana" plus: All These Years • Consequences • In the Dark • Inside Out • Into It • Never Be the Same • Real Friends • She Loves Control • Something's Gotta Give.
00268761 P/V/G......................$17.99

ARIANA GRANDE – MY EVERYTHING

This sophomore solo effort from the Nickelodeon TV star turned R&B songstress reached #1 on the Billboard® 200 album charts and has produced several popular hits. A dozen tracks are featured in piano/vocal/guitar arrangements: Be My Baby • Best Mistake • Break Free • Break Your Heart Right Back • Hands on Me • Intro • Just a Little Bit of Your Heart • Love Me Harder • My Everything • One Last Time • Problem • Why Try.
00146042 P/V/G......................$17.99

NIALL HORAN – FLICKER

This debut solo effort from One Direction's Niall Horan debuted at the top of the Billboard® 200 album charts. Our piano/vocal/guitar folio includes 13 songs from the album: Fire Away • Flicker • Mirrors • On My Own • On the Loose • Paper Houses • Seeing Blind • Since We're Alone • Slow Hands • This Town • The Tide • Too Much to Ask • You and Me.
00255614 P/V/G......................$17.99

IMAGINE DRAGONS – EVOLVE

This 3rd studio album by Nevada rock band Imagine Dragons was released in the summer of 2017 and reached #2 on the Billboard® 200 album charts. Our matching folio includes piano, vocal & guitar arrangements to the singles "Believer" and "Thunder" as well as 9 moresongs: Dancing in the Dark • I Don't Know Why • I'll Make It Up to You • Mouth of the River • Rise Up • Start Over • Walking the Wire • Whatever It Takes • Yesterday.
00243903 P/V/G......................$17.99

MAROON 5 – RED PILL BLUES

Maroon 5 keeps churning out the hits with their sixth studio album, this 2017 release led by the single "What Lovers Do" featuring Sza. Our songbooks features piano/vocal/guitar arrangements of this song and 14 more: Best 4 U • Bet My Heart • Closure • Cold • Denim Jacket • Don't Wanna Know • Girls like You • Help Me Out • Lips on You • Plastic Rose • Visions • Wait • Whiskey • Who I Am.
00261247 P/V/G......................$17.99

P!NK – BEAUTIFUL TRAUMA

This 7th studio album from pop superstar Pink topped the Billboard® 200 album charts upon its release in 2017 led by the single "What About Us." Our matching folio features this song and a dozen more for piano, voice and guitar: Barbies • Beautiful Trauma • Better Life • But We Lost It • For Now • I Am Here • Revenge • Secrets • Whatever You Want • Where We Go • Wild Hearts Can't Be Broken • You Get My Love.
00255621 P/V/G......................$17.99

ED SHEERAN – DIVIDE

This third studio album release from Ed Sheeran topped the Billboard® 200 album charts upon its March 2017 release, led by the singles "Castle on the Hill" and "Shape of You." Our matching folio includes these two hits, plus 14 others: Barcelona • Dive • Eraser • Galway Girl • Hearts Don't Break Around Here • New Man • Perfect • Save Myself • What Do I Know? • and more.
00233553 P/V/G......................$17.99

SAM SMITH – THE THRILL OF IT ALL

Smith's sophomore album release in 2017 topped the Billboard® 200 album charts. This matching folio features 14 songs: Baby, You Make Me Crazy • Burning • Him • Midnight Train • No Peace • Nothing Left for You • One Day at a Time • One Last Song • Palace • Pray • Say It First • Scars • The Thrill of It All • Too Good at Goodbyes.
00257746 P/V/G......................$19.99

TAYLOR SWIFT – REPUTATION

Taylor's 2017 album release continues her chart-topping success, debuting on the Billboard® 200 chart at number 1, led by the first singles "Look What You Made Me Do" and "...Ready for It." Our songbook features these 2 songs plus 13 more arranged for piano and voice with guitar chord frames: Call It What You Want • Dancing with Our Hands Tied • Delicate • Don't Blame Me • Dress • End Game • Getaway Car • Gorgeous • I Did Something Bad • King of My Heart • New Year's Day • So It Goes... • This Is Why We Can't Have Nice Things.
00262694 P/V/G......................$17.99

HAL•LEONARD®

Contents, prices, and availability subject to change without notice.

For a complete listing of the products we have available, visit us online at **www.halleonard.com**